POLICE DOGS

By Sara Green

BELLWETHER MEDIA • MINNEAPOLIS, MN

Jump into the cockpit and take flight with Pilot books. Your journey will take you on high-energy adventures as you learn about all that is wild, weird, fascinating, and fun!

This edition first published in 2014 by Bellwether Media, Inc.

No part of this publication may be reproduced in whole or in part without written permission of the publisher. For information regarding permission, write to Bellwether Media, Inc., Attention: Permissions Department, 5357 Penn Avenue South, Minneapolis, MN 55419.

Library of Congress Cataloging-in-Publication Data

Green, Sara, 1964-
  Police dogs / by Sara Green.
    pages cm. – (Pilot: Dogs to the rescue!)
  Includes bibliographical references and index.
  Summary: "Engaging images accompany information about police dogs. The combination of high-interest subject matter and narrative text is intended for students in grades 3 through 7"–Provided by publisher.
  ISBN 978-1-60014-957-3 (hardcover : alk. paper)
  1. Police dogs–Juvenile literature. I. Title.
  HV8025.G7344 2014
  363.28–dc23
                                                    2013007812

Printed in the United States of America, North Mankato, MN.

TABLE OF CONTENTS

A POLICE HERO

It was a Friday night in Vancouver, Canada. Teak, an eight-year-old German Shepherd, was on police duty with his **handler**, Officer Derrick Gibson. Suddenly, the team received a call about a robbery at a gas station. The partners raced to the scene.

The robber ran out of the gas station before Teak and Gibson arrived. But he did not get far. Teak and Gibson **tracked** him to a nearby neighborhood. At first, Gibson held on to Teak's leash. He gave the robber a chance to **surrender**. When the robber refused, Gibson released Teak and commanded him to grab the robber with his teeth. Teak brought the robber to the ground, but the robber fought back. He stabbed Teak in the neck with a knife!

When the robber was under control, Gibson rushed Teak to a **veterinarian**. Teak needed 30 stitches to close the wound. In time, Teak completely recovered. He retired from the police force a canine hero.

TO PROTECT
AND SERVE

KEEP AWAY
POLICE DOG

Police dogs are valued members of police departments all over the world. They help officers fight crime and save lives. In the early 1900s, police dogs appeared on the scene in the United States. For decades, their numbers remained small. In the 1970s, police dog training improved. Police forces around the country began to include dogs on their teams. Today, thousands of canine officers are on the job every day.

Police dogs are trained to do specific jobs. Tracking dogs use their powerful sense of smell to find **suspects**. They follow scent trails on the ground and in the air. **Detection** dogs use their sense of smell to sniff for bombs, weapons, and illegal drugs. **Cadaver** dogs are trained to find dead bodies. Many police dogs help police officers maintain order. They guard suspects or help keep crowds under control.

The German Shepherd and the Belgian Malinois are the most common police dogs. These breeds are intelligent, strong, and loyal. Their size makes them well suited for police work. They must climb stairs, jump in and out of cars, and run fast. Often, smaller breeds do not have enough **endurance** to handle the demands of the job. Other large breeds, like Collies, are not aggressive in the way police dogs need to be.

Some breeds are also used for specific jobs. Bloodhounds search for missing people. Beagles sniff baggage in airports. They find **contraband** meat, fruits, and vegetables arriving from other countries.

Be Aggressive

Police dogs are trained to be aggressive only on command. Most handlers warn suspects before they set dogs loose. Suspects often surrender instead of running or fighting.

Breeds of Police Dogs

German Shepherd

Belgian Malinois

Bloodhound

Beagle

Profile: German Shepherd

Intelligence
The German Shepherd is the third smartest dog breed. The dog will obey new commands almost immediately.

Size
Height: 22 to 26 inches (56 to 66 centimeters)

Weight: 50 to 95 pounds (23 to 43 kilograms)

Sensitive Nose
The dog can detect a teaspoon of sugar in a million gallons of water. This is equal to two Olympic-sized swimming pools.

Speed
A German Shepherd can reach a speed of 32 miles per hour (51 kilometers per hour), which is much faster than humans can run. This helps the dog catch fleeing suspects.

TRAINING FOR THE FORCE

Police departments get dogs from a variety of places. Some dogs come from rescue shelters or are donated by their owners. However, most police departments use dogs that have been specifically raised for police work. Many of these dogs come from training programs in Europe. European countries such as Germany and the Netherlands have long histories of training police dogs.

Before police dogs come to the United States, they go through special training and earn international **certification**. The dogs learn commands in the language of the country where they were trained. American police officers often continue to give the dogs commands in these European languages. American police forces are glad to have *ein braver Hund*. This means "a good dog" in German!

Bark and Hold

Some police dogs learn to "bark and hold" to capture suspects. The dogs often catch up to suspects before the other officers. They circle around the suspect and bark repeatedly until the rest arrive.

Scent Detectors

Dogs can recognize one certain scent among many others. Some drug dealers wrap drugs in towels soaked with perfume to hide the smell. Police dogs find the drugs anyway.

Police dog training often begins when the dogs are puppies. First, the dogs learn **obedience skills** and good manners. They learn to respond to their handler's voice commands and hand signals. Next, the dogs learn **agility skills**. These include climbing ladders, jumping over walls, and crawling through dark tunnels. Finally, dogs are trained for specific jobs.

Detection dogs learn to sit still when they find bombs and other dangerous objects. This is called a **passive response**. The dog alerts the handler but does not accidentally cause the bomb to explode. Dogs also learn how to give **active responses**. They dig in places where they smell drugs. They bark when they find people or bodies. Police dogs always earn a reward for their work. For many, this means getting to play with a favorite toy!

A COMMITTED TEAM

Police dogs and handlers work closely as a team. They stay together 24 hours a day, seven days a week. They learn to trust each other and understand each other's movements. They protect each other from danger. Every week, the team spends up to eight hours training to keep their skills sharp. Most dogs spend their entire career with only one handler.

When off duty, police dogs relax at home with their handlers. They are also allowed to play with the handler's family and friends. Sometimes the team visits local schools. The dogs demonstrate their skills and the officers answer questions about police work. Children learn about the important work police dogs do in their communities.

OFFICERS IN UNIFORM

Police dogs wear official badges and have uniforms of their own. Bulletproof vests protect many from gunshots. Police dogs are often sent into buildings alone. Some wear special cameras mounted on their backs or heads. They may also have tiny radios. These allow handlers to see what the dogs see and give them commands from a different location.

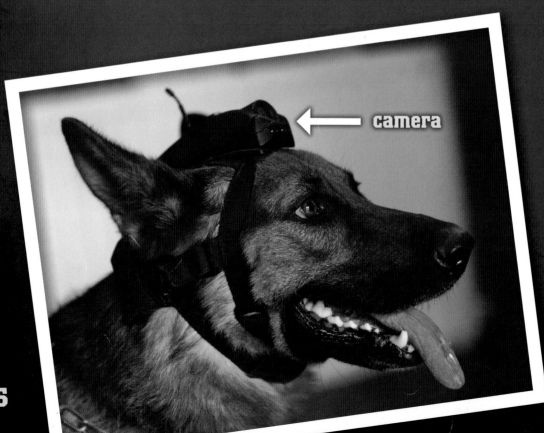

camera

K-9 Unit
A police dog and its handler form a K-9 unit. "K-9" comes from the word canine, which is another word for dog.

bulletproof vest

Police dogs are considered officers of the law. Judges severely punish people who hurt police dogs. Those found guilty of such a crime must pay large fines or go to prison. Police dogs killed in the line of duty receive a funeral ceremony with full police honors. Police officers gather from near and far to honor a fallen canine companion.

RETIRED POLICE DOGS

Most police dogs **retire** when they are 8 to 10 years old. At this age, they cannot handle as much physical activity. Their senses can fade, and they need to rest more. Retired police dogs usually live with their handlers for the rest of their lives. They are treated like a regular family pet. If handlers cannot keep their dogs, police departments find loving homes for them. Many families are happy to adopt a retired police dog.

Retired police dogs sometimes have special needs. Many older dogs can still become aggressive at times. Some require extra care from veterinarians due to injuries or illnesses. Only people who have a lot of experience with dogs should adopt a retired police dog. Under good care, these heroic dogs will enjoy their golden years as guards, playmates, and loyal companions.

DEPUTY KENZO

In the summer of 2012, a nine-year-old German Shepherd named Kenzo made the news in Florida. The police dog and deputy for the Palm Beach County sheriff's department saved the lives of two police officers. But he nearly lost his own.

Kenzo and the officers were chasing a dangerous man through a mobile home park. Suddenly, the man aimed his gun at the officers. Kenzo rushed toward the gunman and put himself between the officers and the gun. The gunman pulled the trigger and fired. The brave police dog was hit with two bullets, but he survived the attack. He was rushed to a veterinary clinic for emergency surgery.

After two months of rest, Kenzo recovered. He returned to the sheriff's department a hero. For his bravery, Kenzo was awarded a Medal of Honor and a Combat Star. These are two of the highest police honors in the United States!

GLOSSARY

active responses—reactions that include an action; digging is an active response.

agility skills—skills that require quick, flexible movements

cadaver—a dead body

certification—the process that recognizes that a dog has mastered specific job skills

contraband—items that are illegally brought into or taken out of a country

detection—identifying something that is hidden

endurance—the ability to do something for a long time

handler—a person who is responsible for a highly trained dog

obedience skills—skills that include sit, stay, come, and down

passive response—a calm, quiet reaction; sitting still and staring is a passive response.

retire—to stop working

surrender—to give up

suspects—people thought to be guilty of a crime

tracked—followed a trail to find someone or something

veterinarian—a doctor who treats animals

TO LEARN MORE

AT THE LIBRARY

Bozzo, Linda. *Police Dog Heroes*. Berkeley Heights, N.J.: Enslow Publishers, 2011.

Hoffman, Mary Ann. *Police Dogs*. New York, N.Y.: Gareth Stevens Pub., 2011.

Miller, Marie-Therese. *Police Dogs*. New York, N.Y.: Chelsea Clubhouse, 2007.

ON THE WEB

Learning more about police dogs is as easy as 1, 2, 3.

1. Go to www.factsurfer.com.

2. Enter "police dogs" into the search box.

3. Click the "Surf" button and you will see a list of related Web sites.

With factsurfer.com, finding more information is just a click away.

INDEX